Zion Oil & Ga
Basin. The Un
March 2010 re
recoverable oi
in the Levant b...
USGS REPORT FS10-3014

"Prophetically, I believe oil will be found on Zion's leases. I do know that this is just the right prophetic time for these discoveries to be made ... I can barely wait to see what will happen next."
HAL LINDSEY

"Dear John, I will continue to pray earnestly for the success and unlimited prosperity of Zion Oil in Israel ... I believe you have been called to the kingdom, 'For such a time as this.'"
PASTOR JOHN HAGEE

"Two major oil companies have been formed to explore oblique references to oil found in the Bible .... John Brown, an evangelical Christian and founder and chairman of Zion Oil and Gas, believes that there is indeed oil in Israel ...."
DR DAVID JEREMIAH

"Epicenter ... predicts this future headline: 'ISRAEL DISCOVERS MASSIVE RESERVES OF OIL, GAS.' ... based on prophecies in Deuteronomy that specifically indicate that "oil" and "hidden treasures" under the sea and the sands will be found in Israel in the last days of history. It is also based on the prophecies of Ezekiel 38 & 39 indicating that Israel will be significantly prosperous in the last days ...."
JOEL ROSENBERG (Epicenter blog, August 18, 2010)

"This is such a vital, vital thing; we shouldn't be surprised at all that God would save this for the end times and that God would save it for his chosen people Israel. We need to pray for John Brown, for Zion Oil and for all the people that are involved in this."
MARCUS LAMB, DAYSTAR TELEVISION NETWORK

True Potential Publishing, Inc.
PO Box 904
Travelers Rest, SC 29690
email: info@tppress.com
website: http://tppress.com

Scripture quotations in this volume are from the King James Version of the Bible unless specifically credited to another source.

ISBN: 978-0-9823059-8-0

LCCN: 2010927887

Printed in the United States of America

THE OIL OF ISRAEL

PROPHECY BEING FULFILLED

(ISAIAH 48:3)

JOHN BROWN

Romans 12:6

"For the vision [the oil] is yet for an appointed time, but at the end it shall speak, and not lie: though it tarry, wait for it; because it will surely come, it will not tarry."

(Habakkuk 2:2-3)

"The secret things belong unto the LORD our God: but those things which are revealed belong unto us and to our children for ever, that we may do all the words of this law."

(Deuteronomy 29:29)

"Remember that thou magnify his work [the oil], which men behold."

(Job 36:24)

This book is dedicated first and foremost to God's faithfulness to His Word (Psalm 138:2) and to his chosen people (Genesis 12:1-3) and secondly to Joan, my wife, who faithfully endured these 29 years with me and lastly to the memory of Jim Spillman.

> *And I heard a voice from heaven saying unto me, "Write, Blessed are the dead which die in the Lord from henceforth: Yea, saith the Spirit, that they may rest from their labors; and their works do follow them."*
>
> (Revelation 14:13)

John M. Brown (Proverbs 25:2)
Zion Oil & Gas, Inc.
Chairman/Founder

TABLE OF CONTENTS

PREFACE

Dear Friends of Zion,

As I begin to write this introduction for this book, I feel compelled to quote a Jewish Rabbi who very profoundly and meekly said, *"with Faith there are no questions, and without Faith, there are no answers."* I do not pretend to have the spiritual insight of these men of God; Jim Spillman, Hal Lindsey, Pastor John Hagee, Marcus Lamb, Rabbi Jonathan Bernis, Joel Rosenberg, Dr. David Jeremiah and Frederick Brotherton Meyer, so I have quoted these men of faith and have used the Bible verses as **I believe God** gave them to me (Psalm 32:8).

> *All scripture is given by inspiration of God, and is profitable for doctrine, for reproof, for correction, for instruction in righteousness. That the man of God may be perfect, thoroughly furnished unto all good works.*
>
> (2 Timothy 3:16-17)

Knowing this first, that no prophecy of the scripture is of any private interpretation. For the prophecy came not in old time by the will of man: but holy men of God spake as they were moved by the Holy Ghost.

(2 Peter 1:20-21)

So, why did God choose Zion to discover the oil in Israel? The answer is I don't know why, but He did, and **I believe** I was told by God that it was to fulfill His promises to Israel (Isaiah 14:24) (Zechariah 1:17) and to bless the body of Christ. (Isaiah 23:18 NIV) and Zion Oil only exists because of God's faithfulness to Israel (Psalms 36:5, 89:1-5) and not because of my faith (Isaiah 25:1).

I believe the promise of Israel's oil begins in Genesis 49:1: *"and Jacob called unto his sons, and said, gather yourselves together, that I may tell you that which shall befall you in the last days."* In verses 22-26, he speaks of blessing Joseph's land with the *"blessings of the deep that lieth under and they shall be on the Head of Joseph."* Then in verse 28, Jacob proceeded to bless the twelve tribes of Israel.

In Deuteronomy 33:1, Moses also spoke to

confirm this, *"and this is the blessing, wherewith Moses the man of God blessed the children of Israel before his death."* In verse 4 *"Moses commanded us a law, even the inheritance of the congregation of Jacob."* In verses 13-16 Moses speaks of Joseph again and that his land would be blessed *"for the deep that coucheth beneath"*; I believe these scriptures speak prophetically of the most precious things (meged) of the earth (oil) and again, just like Jacob's prophecy, the blessing will be found *'on the Head of Joseph'* (see map on page 75).

The blessings on Joseph's land are based on God's promises in which He prophesied through both Jacob and Moses that the blessings lies *deep* beneath the land and on the head of Joseph; Jacob blesses both of Joseph's sons. (Genesis 49:22-26; Hebrews 11:21) and Moses again blessed both sons of Joseph, Manasseh & Ephraim, and the land (Deuteronomy 33:13-16).

When we celebrated the Ma'anit #1 well dedication on April 3, 2005, Rabbi Yittzhak Schwartz, as part of his blessing for Zion, read this scripture:

They shall call the people unto the

mountain; there they shall offer sacrifices of righteousness: for they shall suck of the abundance of the seas, and of treasures hid in the sand.

(Deuteronomy 33:19)

Of the many scriptures I have read, those which spoke a Rhema word to me about the oil of Israel were in Deuteronomy 33:13-16 and 24, when Moses spoke about the tribe of Asher who would *'dip his foot in oil'* on the *'head of Joseph'* and the biblical map confirming these verses to me, which was given to me in 1983 by A.C. Sorelle in Israel while he was drilling the Asher-Atlit well. This map was from a 1976 Bible printed by Zondervan Corporation (see appendices page 75).

My faith journey began in January 1981 when I was saved (see page 73, my testimony). Several months after my 'born again' experience, God sent Jim Spillman to Zion Temple, which at that time was in Clawson Michigan, where the pastor was Leonard Gardner, to share the revelation that God had given to him about the oil of Israel. This was before his book, The Great Treasure Hunt was written and first published in April of 1981. I believed then and now I know that the purpose of Jim's visit to Zion

Temple was to deposit the Vision in my heart to discover the oil of Israel. I want it to be perfectly clear, **I believe** that I was created (Isaiah 46:3,4), saved and chosen by God to fulfill these prophecies and that God alone will receive all the glory (Psalm 145:3-6) by these prophecies being fulfilled (Psalm 83:18; 86:10) and not to me or Zion Oil & Gas because all I am is His unprofitable servant and have only obeyed God and by faith followed Him on this twenty-nine year faith journey (Luke 17:10).

I guess I don't really know why it should be so surprising to us believers that God's Word is true and what will happen in Israel after the oil is found in the last days is only confirming what the Bible says in Deuteronomy. 33:4: *"Moses commanded us a law, even the inheritance of the congregation of Jacob."* In Deuteronomy 34:10 it is written that, *"And there arose not a prophet since in Israel like unto Moses, whom the LORD knew face to face."* Amos 3:7 tells us, *"Surely the Lord God will do nothing, but he revealeth his secret unto his servants the prophets."* And 1 Kings 8:56 states:

> *Blessed be the LORD that hath given rest unto his people Israel, according to all that he promised: there hath not*

> *failed one word of all his good promise, which he promised by the hand of Moses his servant.*

God has promised many such blessings for His people and its impossible for me even to begin to list them all, but He is a faithful God (Psalm 119:89-90) and if you are to receive His promises you must believe and trust Him *"by faith"* that He is able to keep all of His promises (Hebrews11:6).

I was in Israel in May of 1983 when God spoke to me these verses in 1 Kings 8:41-43:

> *Moreover concerning a stranger* [John Brown], *that is not of thy people Israel, but cometh out of a far country for thy name's sake; (For they shall hear of thy great name, and of thy strong hand, and of thy stretched out arm;) when he shall come and pray toward this house; Hear thou in heaven thy dwelling place, and do according to all that the stranger calleth to thee for: that all people of the earth may know thy name, to fear thee, as do thy people Israel; and that they may know that this house, which I have builded, is called by thy name*

"By faith" I believed that *"all"* also must include petroleum oil, so I prayed for the oil of Israel *"by faith"* (John 14:14; Romans 10:17) and I have never doubted that God heard my prayer and would keep His promises to me (Hebrews11:1) and I must encourage you all to trust Him and to gently rebuke you as well. God is faithful so when we doubt Him and don't believe His Word, then what we are saying is that He is not being truthful and is lying to us! (Psalm 40:10) While these are blunt words but it nevertheless is true if we doubt His faithfulness and do not trust Him to perform His Word (Hebrews 6:11-15). God plainly calls unbelief and doubt sin (Romans 14:23) and when the children of Israel disobeyed God and did not believe Him, they paid a severe price (Deuteronomy 1:21-46; 2:15) and we are all called to walk by faith and not by sight (2 Corinthians 5:7). The Bible is full of examples of men who had victorious faith; Abraham, Joshua, Caleb, Jonathan, David, Jehosophat, Job; the list is endless. *"Who through faith subdued kingdoms, wrought righteousness, obtained promises, stopped the mouths of lions."* (Hebrews 11:33) In Chapter 11 of Hebrews which is called the hall of Faith, other men like Abel, Enoch, Noah, Isaac, Jacob, Joseph, Moses and

many others (Hebrews11:29-32) also trusted and obeyed God by faith to fulfill His plan to build the Kingdom of God. Quite frankly, we as believer's should never doubt God, His Word or His promises because our doubt and unbelief **DO NOT** honor God!

If you want to increase your faith, then you must spend time reading His Word (Romans 10:17) and remember that Faith without works is also dead (James 2:14-25) and you cannot receive these promises without you and your faith being tested first (James 1:3; Psalm 105:19).

This book is being written by faith in July 2010 based on God's instructions to me to write a book (Jeremiah 30:2) and to share the Vision (Habakkuk 2:2-3) and before the oil is flowing in Israel. God also told me that after the oil is discovered many more Prophetic visions, which are all written in God's Word, will begin to happen and I am to share these scriptures with you all in (Ezekiel 12:21-28).

John M. Brown
Zion Oil & Gas, Inc.
Chairman/Founder

CHAPTER 1

TRUE BIBLICAL FAITH

So then, what is Biblical Faith? The Bible defines this for us in Hebrews 11:1. ***"Now Faith is being sure of what we hope for and certain of what we do not see."*** And true faith not only believes it but knows it and expects it will happen.

"So then, faith comes by hearing, and hearing by the word of God." (Romans 10:17)

"**BY FAITH**" I received this Blessing and Prophecy from the Rabbi Eliezer Berland, the Dean of the Shuvu Banim Yeshiva in Jerusalem. Rabbi Berland is one of the leading rabbis of the Bratzlav Hassidic court, numbering scores of thousands around the world. The Bratzlav Hassidic court is one of the leading Hassidic movements today, both in and outside of Israel.

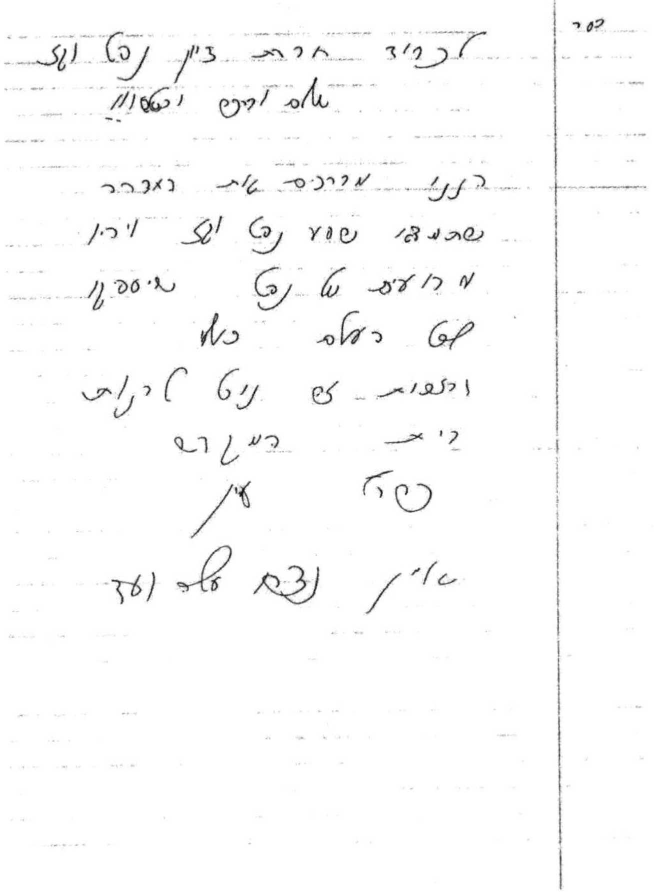

בס"ד

לכבוד חברת ציון נפט וגז
שלום וברכה וישועה!!

הננו מברכים אותם בברכה
שתמצאו שפע נפט וגז ויהיו
מרווחים של נפט שיספיק
לכל העולם כולו
[illegible] עם נפט [illegible]
כי [illegible] [illegible]
[illegible]
[illegible]

TRANSLATION OF THE BLESSING OF RABBI ELIEZER BERLAND

Given to Zion Oil & Gas, Inc. and John Brown on Monday, Sept. 26, 2005

With Heavens' Help

To the Honored ZION OIL & GAS, Inc.
Greetings, a Blessing and All Good Things, Sela.

By these presents we bless your company that you shall find an abundance of oil and gas and that there shall be naturally flowing fountains of oil that will suffice for the whole world. And by virtue of this, we will be able to build the Temple in a twinkling of an eye.

Amen [so be it] for eternity. Sela.

======

Rabbi Berland is the Dean of the Shuvu Banim Yeshiva in Jerusalem. He is one of the leading Rabbis of the Bratzlav Hassidic court, numbering scores of thousands around the world. The Bratzlav court is one of the leading Hassidic movements today, both in and outside of Israel.

ZION OIL & GAS

MAR 2 3 2006

JOHN BROWN
CHAIRMAN AND FOUNDER

November 10, 2005 *via FedEx*

Rabbi Eliezer Berland
14 Hachoma Hashlishit St.
Jerusalem, 95107 Israel

Dear Rabbi Berland,

I very much enjoyed my last visit with you in Jerusalem, and since you requested I return in January 2006, I am planning on being there the week of January 14th. Why this date? I am assuming this is what G-d had ordained for us because isn't that the week the Torah portion is read for Jacob's blessing? (Genesis 49:28) Would you please advise via e-mail if this is the date that you want me to come or not?

Rabbi, it is also written that G-d would send Gentile believers to those who are Jews (Zechariah 8:20-23) and that we are to be treated as one born among you (Leviticus 19:34), and when we are sent, we are to be given an inheritance among you? G-d also said in both (I Kings 8:41-43) and in (2 Chronicles 6:32,33) that when a stranger comes to Israel that he could pray and that G-d would do "all" that the stranger asks him to do. G-d then said in (2 Chronicles 7:12-16) that he would hear these prayers – Forever.

So, I am requesting that you, as a rabbi, would please honor G-d's promise and grant me my inheritance in the lands of Joseph (Ezekiel 47:22-23) which was promised by G-d through both Jacob (Genesis 49:22-28) and Moses (Deuteronomy 33:13-16).

Respectfully your humble servant,

John Brown

"For the Lord will have mercy on Jacob, and will yet choose Israel, and set them in their own land: and the strangers shall be joined with them and they shall cleave to the house of Jacob". (Isaiah 14:1)

6510 Abrams Road, Suite 300, Dallas, Texas 75231 Phone 214.221.4610 Fax 214.221.6510
EMAIL: JB@ZIONOIL.COM WEBSITE: WWW.ZIONOIL.COM

References and Recommended Readings are:

1. ***Moses: The Journey of Faith*** by Frederick Brotherton Meyer
2. ***Faith for Earth's Final Hour*** by Hal Lindsey (www.hallindsey.com)
3. ***Breaking the Treasure Code: The Hunt for Israel's Oil*** by James R. and Steven Spillman (www.tppress.com)

Biblical Faith will only work when we believe that God will keep His promises to us and then our faith pleases God. Because without faith it is impossible to please Him (Hebrews 11:6) and the more that we learn about God (from His Word) the more our faith grows and we become certain of the promises that He makes to us. True biblical faith is always centered only on God's will and Word and not ever self-centered. It must only be based on our belief, trust, and complete confidence in God and His Word only and not in our faith itself or the object of our faith. The faith life always looks at all things through God's Word and His unlimited ability to work out all things for our good (Romans 8:28). Jesus said to us in Mark 9:23: *"... if thou canst believe, all things are possible to him that believeth."*

The Parable of the Sower (Mark 4:1-20)

The key to understanding scripture is to first read and study the Word of God. *"And He said unto them, know ye not this parable? And how then will ye know all parables?"* (Mark 4:13)

Faith is only possible when we are on God's plan, and we stand on God's promise. It is useless to pray for increased faith until we have fulfilled the conditions of faith. It is equally useless to spend time in regrets and tears over the failures, which are due to our doubt and unbelief (Hebrews 3:7-19). Faith is as natural to right conditions of our soul, as a flower is to a plant. And among those conditions; first, find your place in God's plan, and get on it, and then feed daily on God's promises. When each of these are realized, then faith comes of itself and there is absolutely nothing which is impossible. The believing soul can *"do all things"* with God. *"And Jesus answering saith unto them, 'Have faith in God.'"* (Mark 11:22-24)

And what is this kind of faith? It is not some inherent power or quality in certain men, by virtue of which they are able to accomplish special results unrealized by others. It is, rather, the power of putting self aside so God may work unhindered through us. It is the attitude of our heart which having ascertained the will of God, and being desirous of becoming a vessel for it, goes on to believe and expect that God will work out his purposes through us.

It is, in brief, that desire to serve God which allows Him to use us and we become the channel or vehicle through which He passes to bless mankind. The believer is a God-filled, a God-moved, a God-possessed man; and the work which he does in the world is not his, but God's through him. There are, therefore, these necessary conditions of all true faith:

- The sense of helplessness and nothingness (Romans 12:1-3).
- An absolute assurance of being on God's plan (Psalm 32:8).
- Entire consecration that He will work out his plan in our life (Proverbs 19:21).
- The daily food of promise (The Word) (Psalm 119:130).
- A daring to act, in utter independence of feeling, on a faith which trusts completely in the faithfulness of God (Psalm 37:5).

My Testimony - It All Began in 1981
(Revelation 12:11)

1. Zion is a testimony and a journey of faith, which began for me when I was saved, or born again, in January 1981. This testimony is based only on God's faithfulness to the Jewish people and the Nation of Israel (Genesis 17:1-8). Both of which are covenant promises and will come to pass (I Kings 8:56; Isaiah 25:1) and <u>not</u> because of my faith. It is God's purpose and will for my life to discover the oil of Israel (Isaiah 46:9-11; Exodus 9:16).

2. I was saved <u>by faith</u>. It is a gift of God (Ephesians 2:8, 9) and (Romans 10:8-9).

3. Jim Spillman came to Zion Temple in Clawson, Michigan in February 1981 and taught on *"The Oil of Israel"*; <u>by faith</u> I believed it and <u>*The Great Treasure Hunt*</u>. God used Jim Spillman first in my life to deposit the vision for the oil in my heart.

4. <u>*The Vision Book*</u>, I was told <u>by faith</u> to write the vision (Habakkuk 2:2-3).

5. What the Bible (Word) declares comes only <u>by faith</u> (Romans 10:17).

6. The Bible (Word) speaks to us by faith (Psalm 119:105, 130, 138, 160) and then we must *"by faith"* believe the promise (Hebrews 11:1) and then by faith act on it (James 1:22, 23). We are clearly warned by God about doubt and unbelief (Hebrews 3:7-19) and how a true believer's rest can only be obtained by faith (Hebrews 4:1-12). God wrote this about Abraham who is the father of our faith in (Romans 4:1-25).

   Yet, with respect to the promise of God, he did not waver in unbelief, but grew strong in faith, giving glory to God, and being fully assured that what He had promised, He was able also to perform. (Romans 4:20-21).

7. I then went by faith in 1983 to Israel where God gave me (I Kings 8:41-43) and then by faith:

8. (2 Chronicles 6:32-33) I prayed and asked God by faith for the oil! (Hebrews 11:1) And then by faith I believed I received it (Mark 11:22-24) Since then I have by faith believed it and spoken it and do not doubt it (Hebrews 10:38).

9. God called me full time to pursue the vi-

sion for the oil in December 1985 (Acts 22:14-15). So, by faith I resigned my job from Valeron and moved to Houston, Texas (Hebrews 11:8) and then by faith I was told to write the Vision Book (Habakkuk 2:1-3). I was very concerned that I only write what God has written and was confirmed to me in the Bible. There is a severe penalty if we add to or take away from His Word (Revelation 22:18-19) so I wrote *The Vision Book* by faith only after I received (Jeremiah 23:28-29).

"The Oil of Israel" (Amos 3:7)

Jacob's Blessing was *"The Vision"* (Hebrews11:21). By faith Jacob, when he was dying, blessed both sons of Joseph (Ephraim and Manasseh). In the last days (?) (Genesis 49:1; 22-26 [*key verses25-26*]) Joseph's Land will be blessed with oil. Moses' Blessing (Deuteronomy 33:13-16) confirmed Jacob's blessing for Joseph's Land and Asher's foot (v:24) (see the biblical map and Zion's exploration licenses opposite) The rights of the first born were also given to the sons of Joseph (I Chronicles 5:1-2).

10. By faith I then moved to Houston, Texas-1986 to pursue the vision (Hebrews 11:8;

Nehemiah 2:20). After ten years of various trials and testing (Job 23:10) and just like Moses, I tried very hard in my own strength

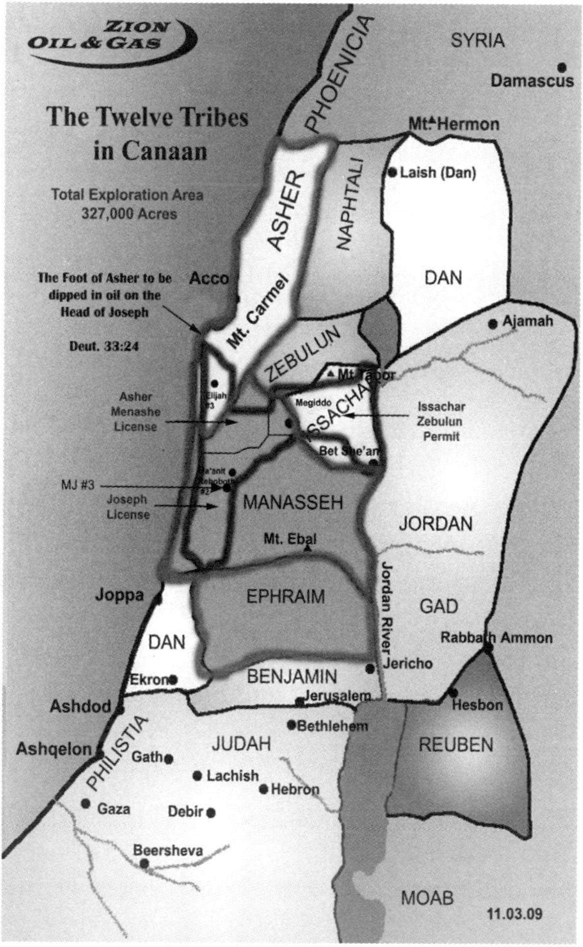

to make the vision come to pass when and how I wanted it to and I failed (Acts 7:24-25) and then God moved me back to Michigan to work with my son, Mark (Isaiah 48:17) and for Joan and I to take care of my mother. (Exodus 20:12)

11. This is quoted from Hal Lindsey's book, Faith for Earth's Final Hour, page 279:

    ... one of life's most difficult things is to keep on trusting the Lord when He delays answering our faith. Yet this is one of the most necessary aspects to develop spiritual faith.

I personally experienced this delay after I returned from Houston to Michigan in 1996. Within the next two years and in 1998, God began to place in my heart once again the desire to become involved in Israel. I really didn't want to go to Israel again because of the previous long trials (15 years), but God gave me the scriptures and told me to go to Israel (Judges 6, 7:15). By faith I then went to Israel and the rest of the story, and Vision, is now being fulfilled, "by faith" in Israel (see www.zionoil.com) and I am to give this testimony *"O give thanks unto the LORD; call upon his name: make known his deeds among the people."* (Psalm 105:1)

CHAPTER 2

THE VISION AND THE CALLING

When first visiting Israel in 1983, I believe that God gave me a scripture (I Kings 8:41-43), a vision (Oil for Israel) and, as a Christian Zionist and New Covenant believer (Isaiah 65:1), the calling to render assistance to the Jewish people and Nation of Israel and to aid them in the Restoration of the Land by providing the oil and gas necessary to help the People of Israel maintain their political and economic independence (Leviticus 19:33,34) (Exodus 6:6-8).

In the Bible, God sovereignly declares that Israel is His chosen people (Exodus 4:22); and we can gain some understanding of God's choice, His vision and purpose by reading (Deuteronomy 7).

As a Christian Zionist, I declare, *"... thy people shall be my people, and thy God my God"*. (Ruth 1:16) And I believe that, as true

Christians, we must all so identify with Israel, as we are all part of the *"wild olive branch"* grafted onto the olive tree by the grace of God (Romans 11). Moreover, I identify with Israel because I share in their struggle and understand a little something of their pain, their confusion, their hope, the media misrepresentation, and the world's disdain of the Jewish people and the nation of Israel - even and perhaps more so today, when Israel appears to be coming under greater criticism for taking those very steps of self-defense which we in America take for granted as our sovereign moral right in defense of ourselves and our interests.

As a believer, I have and can have no doubt that mankind must learn that obedience towards God and His commandments is the key to progress, whether personal or corporate, national or international. Disobedience, on the other hand, can lead only to great difficulty. This too is the story of the Jewish people and the nation of Israel. Indeed, it appears that God's chosen people have ascended to heights and descended to depths far beyond our experience - in both blessings and curses - in progress and disaster.

In considering the history of Israel, however, this principle alone is insufficient to explain the great magnitude of Israel's sufferings. There is another dimension.

Through the centuries and the millennia, Israel has been and continues to be a tangible and visible target for dark spiritual forces which are directed against the living God Himself. No one can touch God; but the Jewish people and the nation of Israel are within reach of those whose hatred is directed against God, and who would foil the fulfillment of His purposes and disrupt His plan for the people of His covenant and the nation of Israel.

This hatred has been manifested time and again throughout the ages. To name only a sampling, there have been the crusades, the inquisition and the pogroms. In the last century, we have seen the Holocaust, as well as the humiliation of, and reneging on, numerous agreements regarding the Land of promise.

Since the re-establishment of the State of Israel in 1948, there have been many wars and many more terrorist attacks. Recently, there has been the Gulf War with scud missiles, threatening chemical mayhem. Then there continues to be, the forced pressure of the 'peace' negotiations and calls of *"land for peace"* - despite the fact that Israel is the only nation on Earth that was created by a sovereign act of God (Genesis 15) and whose borders are defined by God (Numbers 34:1-12). For in (Exodus 32: 13) He said, *"...All of this land which I have spoken of will I give to your descendants and they shall inherit it* ***forever****."*

And when in the summer of 2000, the Prime Minister of Israel indicated that in return for the much prayed for *"peace"*, Israel would be willing to give most of the territory of the Holy Land reconquered in the 1967 War - a war commenced by the Arabs with the declared purpose of destroying Israel - to the Palestinians for an independent state, those very Palestinians rejected the offer, declaring that the Jews had no right to Jerusalem or to the Temple Mount, that the Bible was *"forged"* to show such a connection between the people of Israel and the site of His House, and then they commenced a wave of terrorism, sending human bombs to kill and maim teenagers at discotheques and families at pizza lunches.

Yet the recent events in the land of Israel

notwithstanding, with sorrow and regret, we must admit the truth and confess that the greatest sufferings imposed on the Jewish people throughout history have come from the so-called 'Christian' church and from those confessing the Christian faith. For this we must all ask their forgiveness.

The forces directed against the Jews have misrepresented God and have wrongly interpreted His Word in an attempt to rob Israel of its inheritance which is based on (Genesis 17:7-8) a sovereign promise from God (Exodus 6:4) and an everlasting covenant (Deuteronomy 4:31). Despite the fact that these expressions of evil are totally contrary to God's everlasting covenant, His unchanging nature and purpose, these actions were and continue to be 'justified' by these evil men and nations for their own ends.

But as the Bible declares, God **HAS NOT** forsaken His covenant people (Jeremiah 31:31-40); and, as 'new covenant believers', we are commanded by God in the Bible to stand together with the Jewish people whom the world has abused. As the fulfillment of prophecy is for the Jewish people - for them the realization of their covenant and for them the answer to their prayers of countless generations:

> *And I will plant them upon their land, and they shall no more be pulled up out of their land which I have given them, saith the Lord thy God.* (Amos 9:14-15)

CHAPTER 3

THE SCRIPTURES GIVEN TO JOHN BROWN

THE QUESTION AND THE ANSWER ...The Blessings of the Fathers (Genesis Chapters 17, 27, 49; Deuteronomy Chapters 32, 33)

The economic and political stability of Israel, indeed, its very survival is at stake, not in any small measure because of its dependence on imported oil and gas. The desire to free Israel of such dependence has opened up unexplored areas of Israel and today more sophisticated exploration and drilling techniques than previously used are being utilized to assess the oil potential of those areas.

The State of Israel lies in the heart of the Middle East and is surrounded by areas in neighboring Arab countries which contain the world's largest oil fields. These oil fields are the blessings and posterity which G-d had promised Abraham also for his son Ishmael in (Genesis 17:18-20) and by Isaac's blessing also of his son Esau in (Genesis 27:38-39). The genealogies of Ishmael (Genesis 25:12-18) and Esau (Genesis 36) show that their descendants became the inhabitants of modern day Saudi Arabia and other Arab countries, from Egypt to Iraq and Jordan to Yemen.

The State of Israel, as a national member of the free world and as the only true, stable democracy in the Middle East, strives to find oil to remain independent from outside political pressures.

In 1988, the Government of Israel, acting through the government-owned Oil Exploration Investments Ltd. its affiliates and subsidiaries and geological consultants of renowned international reputation, established the hydrocarbon potential of Israel, and validated the existence of significant quantities of recoverable oil and gas in the Land of Israel, as also exist in the neighboring countries of the Middle East.

Past exploration efforts have yielded several small on-shore discoveries and the recent, significant gas fields off-shore in the Mediterranean Sea. But the 'real potential' still awaits discovery!

Following continued assessment of all geological and geophysical data, renowned petroleum engineers, geologists and geophysicists continue to ask *"... where is the most logical place to drill where we can be sure of tapping those vast reservoirs of oil?"*

Yet, there is an 'ANSWER', and it is found in the most 'overlooked' source of geological information available to mankind today ... the Bible! Archaeologists have found the Bible to be their unerring guide to hidden treasures ... why cannot the geologists utilize the same 'tool' to find this oil?

So we searched the Bible and found numerous passages where, I believe, the Bible in describing the division of the Land of Israel among the sons of Jacob - commencing in Genesis chapter 49. When Jacob on his deathbed summoned His sons and said, *"Gather yourselves together, that I might tell you that which shall befall you in the LAST DAYS"* (49:1); and concluding in Deuteronomy chapters 32 and 33, with Moses' song of praise of G-d and his blessings of the twelve tribes, as G-d prepared him to view the "Promised Land" which HE had given to HIS chosen "Children of Israel" - makes direct reference to the existence of OIL in Israel.

So, friends of Israel, as we begin "The Great Treasure Hunt" may we join hands with the Government of Israel and its people and together look toward and pray for "the discovery of OIL in their homeland, the Land of Israel" and on the "Head of Joseph" as promised in the Torah by the G-d of Abraham, Isaac and Jacob (Genesis 49:25, 26; Deuteronomy 33:13-16).

> *Thus saith the Lord GOD; I will even gather you from the people, and assemble you out of the countries where ye have been scattered, and I will give you the land of Israel.*
>
> (Ezekiel 11:17)

And Israel will be graciously comforted and restored (Micah 7:18-20; Ezekiel 37:15-28).

THE VISION ... The Oil Of Is'ra-el

While visiting Israel with Alger Wolfe in May 1983, John Brown's prayer to the G-d of Abraham, Isaac and Jacob was for oil to be found in Israel. This prayer and G-d's specific instruction to John were based on the biblical portion describing the Dedication of the First Temple in Jerusalem and Solomon's prayers thereat (I Kings 8:22-66).

ONE ... The Prayer

> *Moreover concerning a stranger* [John Brown][1], *that is not of thy people Israel, but cometh out of a far country* [U.S.A.][1] *for thy name's sake: (for they shall hear of thy great name, and of thy strong hand, and of thy stretched out arm); when he shall come and pray towards this house; hear thou in heaven thy dwelling place, and do according to ALL that the stranger calleth to thee for* [Oil for Israel][1]*: that all the people of the earth may know thy name, to fear thee, as do thy people Israel and that they may know that this house, which I have builded, is called by thy name.*
>
> (I Kings 8:41-43)

1 added by J. Brown

TWO ... The Instructions

> *And it shall come to pass, if ye shall hearken diligently unto my commandments which I command you this day, to love the Lord your God and to serve Him with all your heart and with all your soul, that I will give you the rain of your land in his due season, the early rain and the late rain, that thou mayest gather in thy corn, and thy wine, and thine OIL*[2] [the OIL of Israel]. (Deuteronomy 11:13-14)

THREE ... The Evidence

> *Then thou shalt see, and flow together, and thine heart shall fear, and be enlarged; because the abundance of the sea shall be converted unto thee, the forces of the Gentiles shall come unto thee.* (Isaiah 60:5)

These three specific sets of instructions received by John Brown in 1983 from G-d while in the land of Israel, were a consuming 'fire'

2 emphasis added

which has been born by him through the years for the exact purpose that G-d first lit it in his heart! Today, G-d continues to confirm, by HIS Word, the reality of HIS promise when HE also promised...

"For surely there is an end; and thy expectation shall not be cut off." (Proverbs 23:18)

THE CALLING... Tell Them

So, then He told me to "write the vision" (Habakkuk 2:2-3) and then after the oil is discovered, I am to tell them:

> *And the word of the Lord came unto me, saying, "Son of man, what is that proverb that ye have in the land of Israel, saying, the days are prolonged, and every vision faileth? Tell them therefore, Thus saith the Lord God; I will make this proverb to cease, and they shall no more use it as a proverb in Israel; but say unto them, The days are at hand, and the effect of every vision. For there shall be no more any vain vision nor flattering divination with in the house of Israel. For I am the Lord: I will*

speak, and the word that I shall speak shall come to pass; it shall be no more prolonged: for in your days, O rebellious house, will I say the word, and will perform it, saith the Lord God." Again the word of the Lord came to me saying, "Son of man, behold they of the house of Israel say, The vision that he seeth is for many days to come, and he prophesieth of the times that are far off. Therefore say unto them, Thus saith the Lord God; 'There shall none of my words be prolonged any more, but the word which I have spoken shall be done, saith the Lord God.'"

(Ezekiel 12:21-28)

THE PROMISES ... Also Unto the Gentiles
(Leviticus 19:33, 34)

For the prophets foretold that the Gentiles (Isaiah 55:5) would also call upon God and they too would serve him (Zephaniah 3:9) and he would answer their prayers (Isaiah 65:24) and he would save them (Isaiah 52:10) and set them in the land! (Isaiah 14:1) For it is also written:

Also the sons of the stranger, that join

themselves to the Lord, to serve Him, and to love the name of the Lord, to be His servants, every one that keepeth the Sabbath and does not profane it, and all that hold fast to my covenant. Even them will I bring to my holy mountain, and make them joyful in my house of prayer; their burnt offerings and their sacrifices shall be accepted on my altar; for my house shall be called a house of prayer for all peoples. (Isaiah 56:6-7)

A NEW COVENANT PEOPLE ... (Jeremiah 31:31-34)

For God has promised that not only would He honor his First Covenant and would cause the Jews to return (Jeremiah 33:14-26), but that one day He would also make a New Covenant (Jeremiah 31:33-34) and in Hosea 2:23 He said: *"...And I will say to them that were not my people, Thou art my people!"* And they shall say, *"you are my God"* and they will help restore the Nation of Israel and many people would come to the Land of Israel to seek the God of Israel (Zechariah 8:20-23; Isaiah 65:1) and these strangers who dwelt among the people of Israel would also share in the promised inheritance (Ezekiel 47:21-23) and *"... the stranger that dwells with you shall be to you as one born among you."* (Leviticus 19:34) For G-d's promise to Abraham was, *"and in thy seed shall* ***all the nations of the earth be blessed****."* (Genesis 22:18)

So, now we a new covenant people (Deuteronomy 29:12-15) have came to the land of Israel to claim our promised inheritance and to receive the blessings of Abraham. (Galatians 3:6-14). For it is also written, *"... is He the God of the Jews only? Is HE not the God of the Gentiles? Yes, of the Gentiles also,"* (Romans 3:29-30) for G-d hath not cast away HIS people which HE foreknew. *"For if their* [the Jewish people] *being cast away is the reconciling of the world, what will their acceptance be but life from the dead?"* (Romans 11:1-24) Because, *"... that blindness in part has happened to Israel until the fullness of the Gentiles be come in. And so all Israel will be saved."* (Romans 11:24-36) Therefore:

As a Christian, one must recognize that it is written *"... if* [we] *the Gentiles have been made partakers of their* [Israel's] *spiritual things, their* [Gentiles'] *duty is also to minister to them*

[Israel] *in material things."* (Romans 15:27) Because *"the G-d of heaven He will prosper us* [Zion]*"* (Nehemiah 2:20) with the oil of Israel ... so that we, a new covenant people of Zion, will minister and assist 'Israel' in their petroleum and material needs. Because, as touching the election, *"they* [the Jewish People] *are beloved for the sake of the fathers."* (Romans 11:28) And, when they do turn to the Lord, the veil on their hearts will be taken away (2 Corinthians 3:14-16).

THE PURPOSE ... To Receive The Blessings Of Jacob (Genesis 49:1-2 and 22-26)

I believe Zion Oil & Gas was ordained by G-d for the express purpose of discovering oil and gas in the Land of Israel and to bless the Jewish people and the nation of Israel and the body of Christ (Isaiah 23:18 NIV). **I believe** that G-d has promised in the Bible to bless Israel with one of the world's largest oil and gas fields, and this will be discovered in the last days before the Messiah returns and that it will be found on the Joseph License and the Asher/ Menashe License, both being on the Head of Joseph (Genesis 49:1-2 and 22-26):

And Jacob called unto his sons, and said, Gather yourselves together, that I may tell you that which shall befall you in the last days. Gather yourselves together, and hear, ye sons of Jacob; and listen unto Israel your Father ... Joseph is a fruitful bough, a fruitful bough by a well; whose branches run over the wall. The archers fiercely attacked him and shot at him and hated him; but his bow abode in strength, and the arms of his hands were made supple by the hands of the mighty God of Jacob (by the name of shepherd, the Rock of Israel), by the God of thy father who shall help thee; and by the Almighty who shall bless thee, with blessings of the heaven above, blessings of the deep [the Oil of Israel][3] *that lies beneath; blessings of the breasts and the womb. The blessings of thy Father are mighty beyond the blessings of the eternal mountains, the blessings of the everlasting hills* [Oil][3], *they shall be on the head of Joseph, and on the crown of the head of him that was separated from his brothers.*

3 added by J. Brown

... And The Blessing Of Moses (Deuteronomy 33:1, 13-19)

"And this is the blessing which Moses the man of GOD blessed the sons of Israel before his death" (Deuteronomy 33:1)

> *... And of Joseph he said, blessed of the Lord be his land, for the precious things of heaven, for the dew and for the deep* [the Oil of Israel][4] *that coucheth beneath, and for the precious fruits brought forth by the sun, and for the precious things put forth by the moon, and for the chief things of the ancient mountains and for the precious things of primordial hills* [Oil][4] *and fullness thereof, and for the Good will of HIM that dwelt in the bush; let the blessing* [the Oil of Israel][4] *come upon the head of Joseph, and upon the top of the head of him that was separated from his brethren ...*
>
> (Deuteronomy 33:13-16)

> *They shall call the peoples to the mountain; there they shall offer sacrifices of righteousness; for they shall suck of the*

4 added by J. Brown

abundance of the seas, and of treasures [the Oil of Israel][5] *hid in the sand.*

(Deuteronomy 33:19)

THE JOSEPH PROJECT ... The Inheritance (Genesis 48:15-22)

Joseph shall have two portions. And you shall inherit it, one as well as another; that concerning which I lifted up my hand to give it to your fathers; and this land shall fall to you as an inheritance.

(Ezekiel 47:13-14)

And it shall come to pass, that you shall divide it by lot for an inheritance to you, and to the strangers [Gentile believers] *that sojourn among you, who shall beget children among you: and they shall be to you as those born in the country among the children of Israel; they shall have an inheritance with you among the tribes of Israel. And it shall come to pass, that in whatever tribe the stranger may stay, there you shall give him his inheritance, says the Lord GOD.*

(Ezekiel 47:22-23)

---

5 added by J. Brown

CHAPTER 4

NOW BY FAITH ... The Joseph Project

... The Plan ... By Faith (Hebrews 11:1-40)

Zion's approach is somewhat unprecedented ... and that is because of its founder's, John Brown's, FAITH in G-d and HIS promises (Joshua 1:8) and in G-d's faithfulness and ability to perform all HIS Word, as we also walk in the steps of faith as Our Father Abraham walked (Romans 4:11-25). And Jesus said, *"It is written* [Deuteronomy 8:3]*, Man shall not live by bread alone, but by every word of God."* (Luke 4:4)

Now, *"FAITH is the substance of things* [the Oil of Israel][6]*hoped for, the evidence of things not seen."* ... And, it is also written that, *"By FAITH Abraham, when he was tested, offered up Isaac,"* and *"By FAITH Isaac blessed Jacob and Esau concerning things to come"*; *"By FAITH Jacob, when he was dying, blessed*

6 added by J. Brown

each of the sons of Joseph." (Hebrews 11:1-22) G-d's word establishes and so states "... *The JUST shall live by his FAITH"* (Habakkuk 2:4) ... *"But without FAITH, it is impossible to please HIM."* (Hebrews 10:38 and 11:6)

For: We worship by faith as Abel. We walk by faith as Enoch. We work by faith as Noah. We live by faith as Abraham. We govern by faith as Moses. We follow by faith as Israel. We fight by faith as Joshua. We conquer by faith as Gideon. By faith we are patient in suffering, courageous in battle, made strong out of weakness, and are victorious in defeat. We are more than conquerors by our faith seeing "... *there is one God who will justify the circumcised By Faith and the uncircumcised through faith."* (Romans 3:29-30)

So, it is only through faith in JESUS CHRIST that we are saved. *"It is written in the prophets, 'And they shall all be taught by God'* [Isaiah 54:13] *Therefore everyone who hath heard, AND HATH LEARNED OF THE FATHER, cometh unto me."* (John 6:45-51)

From its inception, G-d's plan was born through Faith in G-d's Word into the heart of

John Brown, Zion's founder, and, in all matters concerning Zion, the Word of G-d has been the basis of John Brown's conduct and actions: For it is written:

> *This book of Law shall not depart from your mouth, but you shall meditate in it day and night, that you may observe to do according to all that is written in it.*
>
> (Joshua 1:8)

Consequently, the founder of Zion shall respect and *"Fear God, and keep HIS commandments: for that is the WHOLE duty of man."* (Ecclesiastes 12:13)

When we began again drilling the Ma'anit-Rehoboth Well (MR#2) deeper in April 2009, it was to reach the Permian Zone. "By Faith" **I believed** and so stated publicly that **I believed by faith** that this well would be our discovery well in Israel. However, on April 14, 2010, I was informed that this well would be temporarily suspended. What this means is that I was wrong and I presumed that I knew what G-d would do in 2010 and for this sin of presumption I ask you all for forgiveness (James 4:13-17; Psalm 19:12,13).

However, my faith and belief in the scriptures remains the same and unshaken because I do believe that oil will be discovered in Israel and on the head of Joseph (Genesis 49:28). I'm convinced it will happen someday but I just do not know when (Ecclesiastes 3:1).

> *"Whatsoever the Lord pleased, that did he in heaven, And in Earth, in the seas, and all the deep places."*
>
> (Psalm 135:6)

> *... by the God of thy father who shall help thee; and by the ALMIGHTY who shall bless thee, with blessings of HEAVEN above, blessings of the DEEP* [the Oil of Israel][7] *THAT LIETH BENEATH; ... they shall be on the head of Joseph, and on the crown of him that was separated from his brethren.* (Genesis 49:25-26)

> *... And of Joseph he said, blessed of the LORD be his land, for the precious things of HEAVEN, for the dew and for the DEEP* [the Oil of Israel][6] *THAT COUCHETH BENEATH ... and, for the chief thing of the ancient mountains*

7 added by J. Brown

and for the precious things [Meged] *of the primordial hills* [Oil][8] *and fullness thereof, and for the Good will of Him that dwelt in the bush; let the blessing* [the Oil of Israel][7] *come upon the head of Joseph, and upon the top of the head of him that was separated from his brethren.* (Deuteronomy 33:13-16)

And of Asher he said, Be Asher blessed above sons; let him be acceptable to his brethren, and let him DIP HIS FOOT IN OIL. (Deuteronomy 33:24)

---

8 added by J. Brown

About John Brown

John Brown
Founder and Chairman, Zion Oil & Gas

In 1983, during a visit to Israel, John Brown, spiritually inspired by scripture (1 Kings 8:41-43), dedicated himself to finding oil and gas in Israel; starting the process that led to the Joseph Project. During the next seventeen years he made numerous trips to Israel, hired oil and gas consultants in Israel and Texas, met with Israeli government officials, local exploration companies, and assisted those companies in trying to raise money for oil and gas exploration in Israel. This activity led Mr. Brown to form Zion Oil & Gas, Inc. in April 2000.

John M. Brown the company's founder, has been chairman of the board of directors since its organization in April 2000. He served as CEO until September 2004, and as president of Zion until October 2001. Mr. Brown has extensive management and marketing experience, serving as corporate director of purchasing at GTE Valeron, a subsidiary of GTE Corporation from 1966 to 1986, and as corporate director of procurement at Magnetek Universal, Inc. during 1988-89. Mr. Brown is also a director of M&B Holding Inc. a provider of cement walls and floors for industrial buildings, office buildings and home developers. Mr. Brown attended Fullerton Jr. College and then received a Bachelor of Business Administration degree from Fullerton College, which was awarded to him by a non-accredited correspondence school (1966).

The Joseph Project

- Zion holds 100% of the working interest in their licenses, which means the company is responsible for 100% of the costs of exploration and production. 12.5% of Zion's gross proceeds from the sale of oil and gas belong to the State of Israel as a royalty interest. (I believe this is the tithe, Malachi 3:10)
- Zion holds two Petroleum Exploration Licenses in northern Israel - the 79,000 acre Asher-Menashe License and the 83,000 acre Joseph License for a total of 162,000 acres on the head of Joseph.
- After commercial production Zion will set aside a royalty of 6% for charitable foundations it has established in Israel and Switzerland. (Offerings, Deuteronomy 16:17)
- In 2005, Zion drilled the Ma'anit #1 well on the Ma'anit structure in the Joseph License area. Drilling breaks and shows of hydrocarbons were recorded from 12,000 to the total depth of 15,500 feet. The Ma'anit structure encompasses 7,400 acres.

- From January 2007 to September 1, 2009, Zion Oil & Gas, Inc. was publicly traded on the NYSE Amex, (previously known as the American Stock Exchange) under the symbol "ZN".
- From May 2009 to September 2009, for the Ma'anit-Rehoboth #2, we re-entered the Ma'anit #1 well head to 9,500 feet, 'side-tracked' and drilled to a distance approximately 2,500 feet northeast to a vertical depth of 17,913 feet (5,460 meters) but we did not reach the Permian section of the Paleozoic Age, which was our intended target depth (TD), where **I believe** is - "the blessings of the deep that lies beneath" (Deut. 33:13-16).
- In August 2009, Zion was awarded a preliminary exclusive petroleum exploration permit (the "Issachar-Zebulun Permit") on approximately 165,000 acres onshore Israel (Deut. 33:18,19). As of this writing, a work program is currently underway for the Geophysical Institute of Israel to acquire seismic on the Issachar-Zebulun Permit.
- On September 2, 2009, Zion switched the listing of its common stock and common stock purchase warrants from the NYSE Amex to

the NASDAQ Global Market (NGM). Zion's common stock continues to trade under the symbol "ZN" and Zion's warrants trade under the symbol "ZNWAW".

- In October 2009, the Elijah #3 well was drilled to approximately 10,938 feet when the drill string became stuck. In February 2010, Zion temporarily suspended operations on the Elijah #3 well pending further analysis. As of this writing Zion plans to acquire additional seismic data in order to resolve certain questions regarding the geology surrounding Elijah #3.
- In April 2010, following production and other testing, Zion concluded that commercial quantities of hydrocarbons were not present in the Ma'anit-Rehoboth # 2 (MR#2) well and operations were temporarily suspended.
- As of this writing (August 26, 2010), we have begun drilling a third well at a new drill site (Gen. 26:22) on the Ma'anit Structure. The Ma'anit-Joseph #3 (MJ#3) targets the "deep" Permian geological layer at 5,900 meters(19,000 feet) (Deut 33:13).
- Visit ***www.zionoil.com/rig*** for updates on Zion's drilling and exploration operations.

Zion Oil & Gas
Vision Statement

Comfort and Support to Israel

From its inception, the calling of Zion Oil & Gas has been to assist Israel in the restoration of the Land by finding and producing oil and gas – helping to make Israel politically and economically independent. We see the State of Israel not only as a refuge for Jews, but as the fulfillment of prophecy: "And I will plant them upon their land, and they shall no more be pulled up out of their land which I have given them, saith the Lord thy God." (Amos 9:15)

"Zion" of Many Meanings

The word "Zion" is rich with meaning on many levels. Although it originally referred to the Citadel of Zion on the flank of the lower eastern hill of Jerusalem, in what became known as the City of David, the word was often used by the Hebrew prophets in a much wider sense. "Zion" has been used respectively to refer to the Temple Mount, the entire Land of Israel or even the People of Israel. In Christianity, the word "Zion" represents the heavenly city ruled by God.

The decision to name our company "Zion Oil & Gas" reflects the company's firm belief that our activities will benefit the Land of Israel and its people, as well as working toward the fulfilment of Biblical prophecy concerning "Zion" – in all of its many meanings.

The Blessings of "Joseph", "Asher", and "Issachar and Zebulun" in the "Land of Israel"

And Jacob blessed Joseph (Genesis 49:22-26): "Joseph is a fruitful bough, a fruitful bough by a well; whose branches run over the wall. The archers fiercely attacked him, and shot at him and hated him; but his bow abode in strength, and the arms of his hands were made supple by the hands of the mighty God of Jacob (by the name of shepherd, the Rock of Israel), by the God of thy father who shall help thee; and by the Almighty who shall bless thee, with blessings of heaven above, blessings of the deep that couches beneath, blessings of the breasts and of the womb. The blessings of thy father are mighty beyond the blessings of the eternal mountains, the bounties of the everlasting hills, they shall be on the head of Joseph, and on the crown of the head of him that was separated from his brothers."

And Moses blessed the tribes of the sons of Joseph (Deuteronomy 33:13-17): "And of Joseph he said, Blessed of the Lord be his land, for the precious things of heaven, for the dew and for the deep that couches beneath, and for the precious fruits brought forth by the sun, and for the precious things put forth by the moon, and for the chief things of the ancient mountains, and for the precious things of primordial hills, and for the precious things of the earth, and its fullness, and for the good will of him that dwelt in the bush. Let the blessings come upon the head of Joseph, and upon the top of the head of him who was separated from his brothers."

"And of Asher he [Moses] said, blessed above sons; let him be acceptable to his brethren, and let him dip his foot in oil." (Deuteronomy 33:24.) Of the Land of Israel, Moses sung (Deuteronomy 32:13): "He made him ride on the high places of the earth, and he ate of the produce of the fields; and he made him suck honey out of rock, and oil out of the flinty rock."

And Moses blessed the tribes of Issachar and Zebulun (Deuteronomy 33:18-19): "About Zebulun he said: Rejoice, Zebulun, in your going out, and you, Issachar, in your tents. They will summon peoples to the mountain and there offer sacrifices of righteousness; they will feast on the abundance of the seas, on the treasures hidden in the sand."

Zion's Charitable Foundations

When we are successful in finding commercial quantities of hydrocarbons in Israel, a portion of the revenues from production will go to charities in Israel, the United States and elsewhere in the world. For this purpose, two charitable foundations have been established by us (Lev. 27:30, Deut. 16:17).

Our shareholders, in a resolution passed at the 2002 Annual Meeting, gave authority to Zion's Board to transfer a 3% overriding royalty interest to each of two foundations (to be established in the future).

In Israel, we established the **Bnei Joseph Foundation**. In November 2008, both the Articles of Association and Incorporation Certificate were certified by the Registrar of Amutot, (i.e. the Registrar of Charities), in Israel.

In Geneva, Switzerland, for worldwide

charitable activities, we established the **Abraham Foundation**. In June 2008, the articles of incorporation were executed and filed by the Swiss Notary in the Commercial Registrar in Geneva and in November 2008, the Swiss Confederation approved the Foundation as an international foundation under the supervision of the federal government. In December 2008, the Republic of Geneva and the Federal government of Switzerland issued a tax ruling providing complete tax exemption for the Foundation.

In February 2009, we assigned both (i) a 3% overriding royalty interest to the Bnei Joseph Foundation (in Israel) and (ii) a 3% overriding royalty interest to the Abraham Foundation (in Switzerland). In June 2009, the Israeli Petroleum Commissioner formally approved Zion's transfer of the overriding royalty interests to the respective foundations.

The general application of the funds will be to support projects for the restoration of the land and people of Israel and social, charitable, medical, religious, educational and rehabilitative projects in the United States and internationally.

Since Zion Oil had been drilling in Israel John Brown has received hundreds of letters and phone calls from well wishers, fans and lovers of Israel. Below is a small sample:

Subject: FW: getting involved with Zion

To whom it may concern:

Since 1983, after attending a service by Jim Spillman, my father has been telling me about the visions of oil exploration in Israel. I have followed the efforts closely for many years, and was extremely excited after learning of Zion. I am a dedicated Christian, and believe that the discovery of oil in Israel will play an extensive role in the end times and the fulfillment of scripture. ... Your company and the country of Israel will continue to be in my thoughts and prayers.

Sincerely,

T. N.

Subject: oil and wine

Hi John,

Just wanted to let you know, I believe in what you're doing. I've invested in your company and look forward to seeing what God has in store for you and your company!

The Bible does seem to mention oil in various places, that of the petroleum kind. I've studied this based on your work and that outlined in the Great Treasure Hunt.

One other thing... Thursday morning I'll be a father for the first time! My son's name is Gabriel Asher Kyle! 3 years ago I got an inspired message from God about having a son, with a strong inclination of the name Gabriel after the message. You know that Gabriel announced Jesus coming to Mary, and John the Baptist to Zacharius. Regarding Asher ... I was reading a few names to my wife and she really liked Asher, so knowing that it came from one of the 12 tribes of Israel, I liked it and we went with it! Knowing his name means 'blessing and happy' is great, and bringing this back to Zion and having already had invested with you and your Asher license is very interesting, to say the least!

I believe God has great plans for both Zion Oil and my baby boy!

Take care and God bless,

J. K.

Subject: Oil Blessings

Hello Brother John:

It feels funny sending you an e-mail where we don't know each other at all. Recently at a ministry meeting we were discussing the End Times and

God's plan for Israel. One of the Christian Brothers shared your testimony and talked about Zion Oil & Gas. I was interested in what Gods Word spoke about this blessing and oil as it relates to the blessings spoke about in Gods Word.

To my encouragement I saw something that would change my thinking about today and what will happen tomorrow. Being unemployed recently and having limited finances and no leads for employment, I took a step of faith and purchased five shares of Zion Oil & Gas and as finances are available I will purchase five shares each month.

I recently started my own business to help companies improve quality and follow standards. As you mention on your video, we are held to a higher standard following and obeying the Lord. I believe the Lord directs our steps and I have faith in His outcome for my life. Thank you again for following the Lords direction and stepping out in faith.

God Bless

R. J.

Subject: Thanks and Blessings to Zion Oil

Dear Brittany (John Brown's assistant),

I was so deeply touched by the kindness of your wonderful staff that I met while attending the C.U.F.I. Washington D.C. Conference.

Words cannot describe the leap of joy of the Holy Spirit within me as I beheld your vision and great work you are doing for our beloved Israel and the God of Abraham. Thank you from the bottom of our hearts. I was so melted as they handed me a signed copy of the book as a token to me.

Before I had gone to Washington, I had told my wife that in my heart, I believed that God was going to bless Israel with more oil than any nation, and I couldn't put my finger on it but that it was so real to me. This was before I discovered what you all were doing at the CUFI Wash D.C. It was nice to see that God had put the same thing on many other hearts, and that you all were actually putting legs on the thing. It's nice to have confirmation to let you know that you are not that crazy after all. .You don't know what it meant to us to hear that you all were going to get the oil for God and Israel. We are all rooting for you with prayers and faith.

Please let me know if there is still the availability of giving offerings/investments at an affordable rate that I could consider participating in to bless Israel, bless Zion Oil's efforts, and by the grace of God bring blessing to our church, ministry and family. May God Bless you as you dip your foot in oil and receive the blessings of the deep as you strike oil to the glory of the Lord, to the credit of God's Word, and to bless Israel. We truly appreciate your work in the Lord.

R. C.

"A Question of Faith"

The prophecy of oil for Israel, the vision of John Brown, the mission of Zion Oil & Gas - a sixty minute documentary produced by True Potential Media (www.truepotentialmedia.com) to be released early in 2011.

For more information and to follow the making of ***"A Question of Faith"*** *go to:*
www.faith-documentary.com

JEWS AND CHRISTIANS UNITED FOR ISRAEL™

THE MISSION STATEMENT

The purpose of **JEWS AND CHRISTIANS UNITED FOR ISRAEL** (the "***Association***") is to provide both Jews and Christians with an association through which, together, they can show their support for Israel and stand united against all forms of theological, cultural and political anti-Semitism. Anti-Semitism is an assault on G-d, as well as on the Jewish people.

SCRIPTURAL FOUNDATION

Jews and Christians – come - let us walk by the light of HASHEM! (Isaiah 2:5)

Come let us go up to the Mountain of HASHEM, to the Temple of the God of Jacob, and He will teach us of His Ways and we will walk in His paths. For from Zion will the Torah come forth, and the word of HASHEM from Jerusalem. Isaiah 2:3

Let not the foreigner, who has joined himself to HASHEM, speak, saying, "HASHEM will utterly separate me from His people.". . And the foreigners who join themselves to HASHEM to serve Him and to love the Name of HASHEM to become servants unto Him, all who guard the Sabbath against desecration, and grasp My covenant tightly – I will bring them to My holy mountain, and I will gladden them in My house of prayer; their elevation-offerings and their feast-offerings will find favor on My Altar, for My House will be called a house of prayer for all the people. The word of my Lord, HASHEM/ELOHIM, Who gathers in the dispersed of Israel: I shall gather to him even more than those already gathered to him. (Exiled Jews and many gentiles will rally to the Messiah) *(Isaiah 56: 3-8).*

SPIRITUAL MESSAGE

This Association will carry a message -- a message to the world that the G-d of Abraham, Isaac and Jacob is and the covenants with Israel and the Jewish people are eternal and have never been set aside. The Association will shout out that its blessings are flowing from the G-d of Abraham.

For the times are always difficult for Israel, who has many enemies, and there is another rising tide of anti-Semitism around the world. The new code word for anti-Semitism is anti-Zionism. Anti-Semitism is an assault on G-d, as well as on the Jewish people. The Association must do everything that it can to make Israel strong and deliver the message that we not stand for anti-Zionism and anti-Semitism. Anti-Semitism was and is deeply imbedded in Christian Church doctrine and tradition based upon the chosen people being no longer "Israel" but the Church.

According to Franklin H. Littell in *The Crucifixion of the Jews: The Failure of Christians to Understand the Jewish Experience*, the primary question for the Christian church is where it stands on the survival of the Jewish people and Judaism. With Christian anti-Semitism based upon the superseding or displacement myth of the Jewish people, the restored Israel and the continued existence of the Jewish people are a substantial refutation of the traditional Christian myth about the eventual annihilation, assimilation, or withering away of the Jewish people and Judaism.

If Christians want to understand the very

foundations of their religion, they need to understand what should be their relationship and understanding of the Jewish people, G-d's witnesses on earth, and modern Judaism. Christians need to recognize that their mission of preparing for the coming of the Kingdom of G-d is shared with the Jewish people and the Jewish people have their own fulfillment in faithfulness to the divine covenant promised by G-d in *Genesis*.

Elie Wiesel has commented that "Auschwitz represented a failure, a defeat for 2,000 years of Christian civilization." Wiesel in *Messengers of God, Biblical Portraits and Legends* lamented who among the Christian community actually studies the Word of G-d in which he said.

> *In Jacob's vision of the future, he wept together with his persecuted descendants. And this was how he addressed God: In Your Book, it is written that one may not slaughter an animal and her young on the same day. This law shall not be observed by the enemy; he will kill mothers and their children in each other's presence. I shall not ask You who will observe Your Law; I shall simply ask You to tell me who will study it.*

In his dream Jacob saw a ladder whose top reached into heaven. It still exists. There are those who have seen it, somewhere in Poland, at the side of an out-of-the way railroad station. And an entire people [were] climbing, climbing toward the clouds on fire. Such was the nature of the dread our ancestor Jacob must have felt.

The Christian community does not realize that instead of choosing to assimilate at all costs because of anti-Semitism, Jewish people worldwide continue to renew and intensify their Jewish life and to raise Jewish children. Knowing of the fate to which these decisions may threaten their family and of how little the world really cares, such decisions can only come from faith and trust in G-d.

Judea and Ruth Pearl in *I Am Jewish, Personal Reflections Inspired by the Last Words of Daniel Pearl* said that to be Jewish is to be part of a four-thousand year old community of memory that recognizes what we owe to those who have come before us. The Jewish people are the only people in the world today who still inhabit the same land, embrace the same religion, study the same Torah, speak the same aboriginal language, Hebrew, and hear the same name, Israel, as they did 3,500 years ago.

To the people who say show me proof that G-d exists, I say look to G-d's witnesses on earth, look at the history of the Jewish people after two thousand years of persecution and the Holocaust and you will see proof that G-d exists. The Jewish people live. Israel lives! Judaism lives!

Many evangelical churches still preach a modified form of replacement theology, in which they claim that the world is now in the time of the Church and G-d has set aside the Jews. If there is another Holocaust, then it is to be. They see no purpose in Christian dialogue with the Jewish people, unless the Jews want to accept the Christian message of salvation.

A leading theologian of Christian-Jewish dialogue, Paul M. van Buren, has stated that **if the Christian church is faithful to G-d and His covenant with His people, the proper mission of the Christian church to the Jewish people would be to help Israel to be what it is in the covenant by G-d's election and to help it perform its mission.**

Israel's mission to the world and the Association's guiding mission to the world should be the same - *tzedaka u-mishpat* - the two virtues which were the basis for Abraham's initial election by G-d. I have known, loved and appointed Abraham in order that he commands his children and household after him to observe the way of the Lord, which is to do compassionate righteousness [*tzedaka*] and moral justice [*mishpat*]. This is why G-d promised to make of Abraham a great and powerful nation through whom all the nations of the earth would be blessed. *Genesis 18: 18-19.*

As the natural and spiritual children of Abraham, we must through our decisions radiate this compassionate righteousness [*tzedaka*] and moral justice [*mishpat*] that shows that we are pursuing Israel's mission to the world through the Association. By pursuing Israel's mission, Israel and the world will be blessed. And this is the spiritual message that the Association must deliver.

Radical Islam has picked up the torch of anti-Semitism from the Nazis and Professor Robert S. Wistrich has said that Hitlerism did not die in April 1945 nor was Auschwitz truly "liberated," but this "culture of hatred" has been ignited across the Arab-Muslim world. For radical Islam is not about the territorial or national issue of the Israeli-Palestine conflict, but about the spirit of Nazi ideology in exterminating the Jews.

All citations to the Bible are to the Stone Edition of The Tanach, the Torah/Prophets/Writings: the Twenty-Four Books of the Bible. Brooklyn: Mesorah Publications, Ltd. (2nd ed. Tenth Impress. 2007).

Martin M. van Brauman
Jews and Christians United For Israel
5646 Milton Street, Suite 940
Dallas, Texas 75206
(214) 914-2018
mmvanbrauman@tx.rr.com

Note: the above discussions and message are derived from Mr. van Brauman's upcoming book entitled ***Picking Up the Cross of Jewish Crucifixion: My Discovery of Being a "Remnant" of the Natural Branch of Abraham***, which shall be dedicated to the Brauman family of shoah victims honored at Yad Vashem.

Dear Friends of Zion,

On the following page (72) is a copy of my personal testimony. In Romans Chapters 10 & 11, the scriptures contain Paul's Prayers for Israel and that salvation is open to both the Jew and Gentiles. It clearly states that a remnant of Israel will be saved by an Election of Grace and that G-d himself caused a spiritual blindness to fall on the rest. And we Gentile believers are warned by G-d to not boast against them (Romans 10:11-15). If you will read chapter 11 very carefully, you will see that G-d has a plan for Israel and the Jews in Verse 25 "for I would not, brethren that ye should be ignorant of this mystery, lest ye should be wise in your own conceits; that the blindness in part is happened to Israel, until the fullness of the Gentiles be come in" and in verse 26 "and so all Israel shall be saved: as it is written, there shall come out of Zion the deliverer, and shall turn away ungodliness from Jacob"; but until then we are warned in verse 28 "as concerning the gospel, they are enemies for your sakes: but as touching the election, they are beloved for the fathers sake".

> *"O the depth of the riches both of the wisdom and knowledge of God! How unsearchable are his judgments, and his ways past finding out!"*
>
> (Romans 11:33-36)

John M. Brown
Founder, Jews and Christians United for Israel

June 1983

TO ALL MY FRIENDS AT GTE VALERON

Now it is with deep regret that I must resign from GTE Valeron. However, I am involved in an oil project that God blessed me with in Israel, and now will devote all of my time in the oil business and doing God's work. Most of you are familiar or know of my past when I was hospitalized four (4) times for alcoholism, but this was all changed dramatically in January 1981 when I was "Saved" or "Born Again". These two (2) terms are not from any denomination, but it is from the Bible and can be found in the New Testament in the book of St. John, Chapter 3 verses 3 through7. What these terms mean is that I accepted JESUS CHRIST as my Personal Savior. I can testify that I have sat in churches all my life, but I was not "Saved" or "Born Again".

There is no church membership or denomination or water baptism whereby you are "Born Again" or "Saved", and there is Salvation in no other way but for each person to individually accept JESUS CHRIST as their own personal Savior and Lord of their life. Like St. Paul in the New Testament, I was instantly converted and I believe it was to be a witness for you especially here at GTE Valeron. Please don't misunderstand me, as I am not anything special nor did I earn the Salvation, because it cannot be earned as it is a universal gift of God and available to everyone who wants it.

I now pray that each and every one of you will believe that what happened to me is very real and seek the truth for yourselves. Please don't ignore what God is saying to you through me because it is a clear choice whether you choose JESUS CHRIST as your Personal Savior and receive eternal Salvation, or deny Him and Choose eternal damnation.

I love you all and that is why I'm sending you this.

IN HIS LOVE,

John Brown

Testimony JB

It should be fairly obvious by now that I have written this book entirely **by faith** (Jer. 30:2) (2 Cor. 4:13) and no one should invest in Zion Oil and Gas, Inc. based only on my faith, beliefs and personal interpretation of the scripture. All investments in Zion Oil and Gas, Inc. should be based on both prayer (Isa. 48:17) and only after a very thorough legal and financial review of all of Zion's SEC Filings (www.sec.gov). This book will be given out as a gift to whomever requests it directly from Zion Oil & Gas (www.zionoil.com).

FORWARD LOOKING STATEMENTS: Statements in this communication that are not historical fact, including statements regarding Zion's planned operations, geophysical and geological data and interpretation, anticipated attributes of geological strata being drilled, drilling efforts and locations, the presence or recoverability of hydrocarbons, the sufficiency of cash reserves, ability to raise additional capital, the successful establishment of the drilling subsidiary and the negotiation and execution of definitive agreements with the rig owners, timing and potential results thereof and plans contingent thereon are forward-looking statements as defined in the "Safe Harbor" provisions of the Private Securities Litigation Reform Act of 1995. These forward looking statements are based on assumptions that are subject to significant known and unknown risks, uncertainties and other unpredictable factors, many of which are described in Zion's periodic reports filed with the SEC and are beyond Zion's control. These risks could cause Zion's actual performance to differ materially from the results predicted by these forward-looking statements. Zion can give no assurance that the expectations reflected in these statements will prove to be correct and assumes no responsibility to update these statements.

For more information about Zion Oil & Gas, Inc.
please visit:
www.zionoil.com

To order copies of *The Oil of Israel: Prophecy Being Fulfilled* by John Brown, *The Great Treasure Hunt* by Jim Spillman and *Breaking the Treasure Code: the Hunt for Israel's Oil* and *The Oil of Israel: Prophecy Being Fulfilled*
please visit:
www.tppress.com

ZION OIL & GAS

Zion Oil & Gas

USA

6510 Abrams Road, Suite 300
Dallas, Texas 75231
Phone: 214.221.4610 Fax: 214.221.6510
Email: dallas@zionoil.com

Israel

15 Bareket Street, POB 3138
North Industrial Park
Caesarea 38900 Israel
Phone: +972-(0)4-623 1425 Fax: +972-(0)4-623 1427
Email: israel@zionoil.com

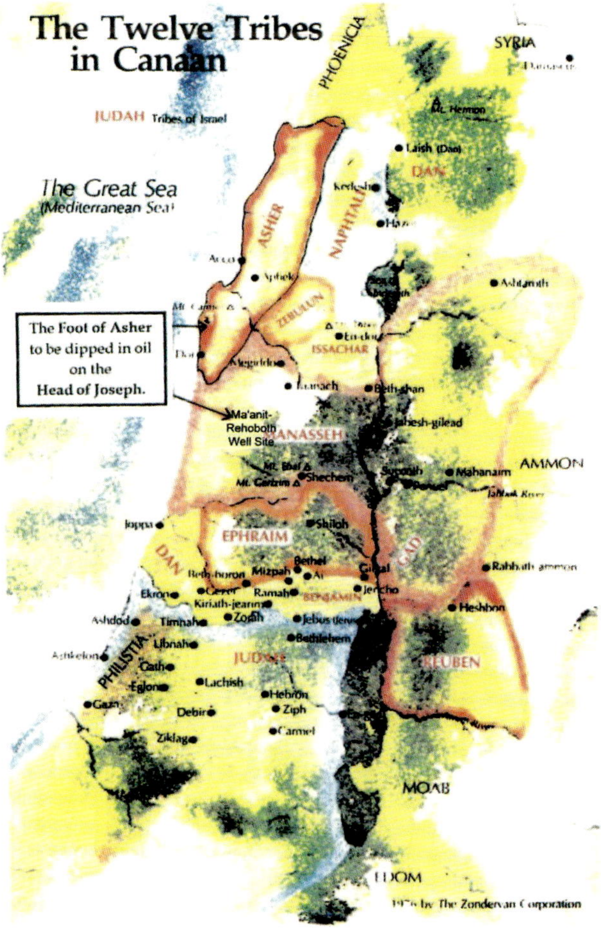

Deuteronomy 33:24

And of Asher he said, "Let Asher be blessed with children; let him be acceptable to his brethren, and let him dip his foot in oil."

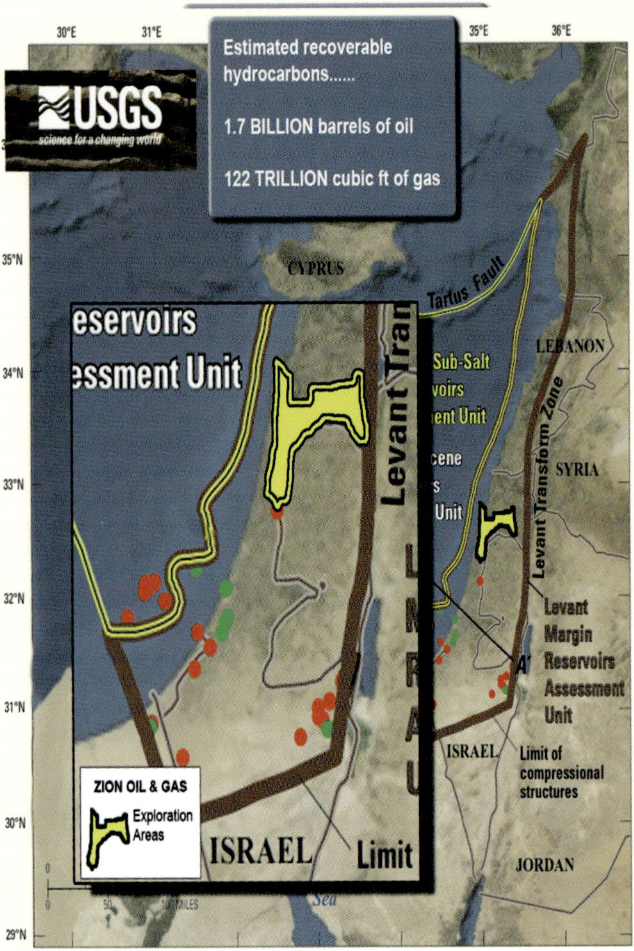

Estimated recoverable hydrocarbons......
1.7 BILLION barrels of oil
122 TRILLION cubic ft of gas
USGS
science for a changing world
CYPRUS
Tartus Fault
LEBANON
SYRIA
ISRAEL
JORDAN
Levant Transform Zone
Levant Margin Reservoirs Assessment Unit
Limit of compressional structures
ZION OIL & GAS
Exploration Areas
Limit

ZION OIL & GAS, INC.

A special company with a special task in a special country

Background

Zion Oil & Gas was formed in 2000 by John Brown, a man of deep Christian faith. The company, which is listed on the NASDAQ exchange (trading symbol **ZN**), explores for oil and gas on two onshore petroleum exploration licenses (the Joseph license and the Asher-Menashe license) covering approximately 162,000 acres between Tel Aviv and Haifa. Zion also has a 165,000 acre permit area (the Issachar-Zebulun Permit Area), so Zion's total petroleum rights exploration area is over 325,000 acres.

Pastor John Hagee with Zion CEO, Richard Rinberg, in Jerusalem

Vision

From the beginning, the calling of Zion Oil & Gas was to assist in the restoration of the Land of Israel by finding oil and gas, helping Israel to become more independent, both economically and politically.

Faith & Science

In the beginning, Zion operated by faith alone, but today it is also based on hard science. Zion's geological team has gathered information from all of the wells drilled in Israel and compiled a country-wide seismic database consisting of 219 seismic sections totaling 2,000 miles, so as to better understand the geology of our exploration areas. In 2005, Zion drilled the Ma'anit #1 well on the Ma'anit structure in the Joseph license area and shows of hydrocarbons were recorded from 12,000 feet to 15,500 feet. Due to mechanical problems, the well was abandoned in June 2007.

2009

In May 2009, we re-entered the wellbore of the old Ma'anit #1 well and then 'sidetracked' (drilled directionally) to a distance approximately 2,500 feet northeast of the present location. This new second well, the Ma'anit-Rehoboth #2, was drilled to a depth of 17,913 feet. After drilling, during swabbing operations, a small quantity of crude oil was retrieved.

In October 2009, the drilling rig moved northwards, to our Asher-Menashe license, to drill our Elijah #3 well. The well is on a ten thousand acre structure and has targets in both the Triassic and the Permian geological layers.

2010

By early February 2010, we had drilled the Elijah #3 well to a depth of 10,938 feet and temporarily suspended drilling operations

Zion's Technical Committee (Bill Ottaviani, Zion's President and COO - not shown). Left to Right: Mr. Victor Carrillo (Chairman of the Texas Railroad Commission), Dr. Eliezer Kashai, Dr. Yehezkel Druckman and Mr. Forrest Garb

following unsuccessful efforts to retrieve a stuck pipe. We have recently acquired additional field seismic data intended to resolve certain questions regarding the geology of the area surrounding the Elijah #3 well.

Hal Lindsey visits Zion's Ma'anit drill site in Northern Israel

In August 2010, we began drilling the Ma'anit-Joseph #3 well, in our Joseph License area. Drilling operations are planned to test the Permian geological formation and are expected to last approximately six months. By the end of September 2010, we were drilling at a depth of 4,750 feet.

The Future

We plan to complete the drilling of the Ma'anit-Joseph #3 well, complete the drilling of the Elijah #3 well, establish a drilling subsidiary company, carry out further scientific investigation work in the field and implement our multi-well drillin program just as fast as practicable.

If you want to see the latest news regardin Zion, please visit our website at

www.zionoil.com

FORWARD LOOKING STATEMENTS: Statements in this communication that are not historical fact, including statements regarding Zion's planned operation potential results thereof and potential effects of those results, including the drilling of further wells and the successful establishment of a drilling subsidiar are forward-looking statements as defined in the "Safe Harbor" provision of the Private Securities Litigation Reform Act of 1995. These forward-looking statements are based on assumptions that are subject to significant known and unknown risks, uncertainties and other unpredictable factors, many of which ar

JESUS
LOVES YOU

JESUS
LOVES YOU

JESUS
LOVES YOU

JESUS
LOVES YOU

HOW TO MAKE HEAVEN YOUR HOME

"For God so loved the world, that He gave His only begotten Son, that whosoever believeth in Him should not perish, but have everlasting life." -John 3:16

"For all have sinned and fall short of the glory of God." -Romans 3:23

"If you will confess with your mouth that Jesus is Lord, and believe in your heart that God has raised Him from the dead, you will be saved." -Romans 10:9

"Jesus said 'I am the way, and the truth, and the life; no one comes to the Father, but by me.'" -John 14:6

PRAY THIS PRAYER:
Dear Jesus, I am a sinner. I believe that you died and rose from the dead to save me from my sins. I want to be with you in heaven forever. Jesus forgive me of all of my sins that I have committed against you. I here and now open my heart to you and ask you to come into my heart and life and be my personal Lord and Savior. Amen.

HOW TO MAKE HEAVEN YOUR HOME

"For God so loved the world, that He gave His only begotten Son, that whosoever believeth in Him should not perish, but have everlasting life." -John 3:16

"For all have sinned and fall short of the glory of God." -Romans 3:23

"If you will confess with your mouth that Jesus is Lord, and believe in your heart that God has raised Him from the dead, you will be saved." -Romans 10:9

"Jesus said 'I am the way, and the truth, and the life; no one comes to the Father, but by me.'" -John 14:6

PRAY THIS PRAYER:
Dear Jesus, I am a sinner. I believe that you died and rose from the dead to save me from my sins. I want to be with you in heaven forever. Jesus forgive me of all of my sins that I have committed against you. I here and now open my heart to you and ask you to come into my heart and life and be my personal Lord and Savior. Amen.

HOW TO MAKE HEAVEN YOUR HOME

"For God so loved the world, that He gave His only begotten Son, that whosoever believeth in Him should not perish, but have everlasting life." -John 3:16

"For all have sinned and fall short of the glory of God." -Romans 3:23

"If you will confess with your mouth that Jesus is Lord, and believe in your heart that God has raised Him from the dead, you will be saved." -Romans 10:9

"Jesus said 'I am the way, and the truth, and the life; no one comes to the Father, but by me.'" -John 14:6

PRAY THIS PRAYER:
Dear Jesus, I am a sinner. I believe that you died and rose from the dead to save me from my sins. I want to be with you in heaven forever. Jesus forgive me of all of my sins that I have committed against you. I here and now open my heart to you and ask you to come into my heart and life and be my personal Lord and Savior. Amen.

HOW TO MAKE HEAVEN YOUR HOME

"For God so loved the world, that He gave His only begotten Son, that whosoever believeth in Him should not perish, but have everlasting life." -John 3:16

"For all have sinned and fall short of the glory of God." -Romans 3:23

"If you will confess with your mouth that Jesus is Lord, and believe in your heart that God has raised Him from the dead, you will be saved." -Romans 10:9

"Jesus said 'I am the way, and the truth, and the life; no one comes to the Father, but by me.'" -John 14:6

PRAY THIS PRAYER:
Dear Jesus, I am a sinner. I believe that you died and rose from the dead to save me from my sins. I want to be with you in heaven forever. Jesus forgive me of all of my sins that I have committed against you. I here and now open my heart to you and ask you to come into my heart and life and be my personal Lord and Savior. Amen.